praise for A Most Natural Thing

"How do we learn the elements of air, fire, water, and earth? For some, the first naming may be through a book or through an elementary lesson. The way many learn has the taint of control, as if, in learning a name, we might control those elements, which are distant and external to ourselves. This hybrid memoir defiantly troubles this reasoning; here we learn an elemental resonance and timbre through memory, lyric and its myriad shape, sensorially rich practices of attunement, and the revelation of intuitive knowing. Yes, of course, the Vestal Virgin can be guardian of energetic transformation. Yes, of course, the stone is an ancestor. Yes, of course, the water will change its vibration in accordance with prayer and whispered intentions. Of course, fire is alive. This text, too, is alive with sensuality, heat, longing for home within interpersonal relationships and place, connection across borders, loneliness across time, and a grief that is timeless. Several times in reading the text I found myself completely captivated at the skillful interweaving of the personal, the spiritual, the societal critique, the stake of history on the present day, the illness and how we reach for healing and breath at the altar. This is a text of breath and groundedness, a book that could find an honored place on an altar as centering icon on this truth: we are all elementally connected. How can we hold one another more tenderly with that knowledge, because we must?"

— **Raina J. León,** author of *black god mother this body*

"In a book that asks how humanity can both 'hold such desperate faith' and 'punish [its] dreamers,' Lisbeth White's *A Most Natural Thing* guides readers deep into a world forged with as much indifference as beauty. Combining memoir, historical inquiry, and travel narratives blooming with lyricism and vulnerability, White's prose treads the line between meditation and prayer, navigating the triumphs and complexities of identity, community, and belonging. A trip to Mexico at the start of the COVID pandemic brings to light the toll of emotional loneliness and physical isolation. Standing at the edge of Washington State becomes a reflection on whales and their habitat, and ultimately our callousness toward other creatures. And a summer at the Blue Ridge Mountain range questions the extent to which groups of people are accepted in this country. *A Most Natural Thing* maps out a new literary territory, one that places a profound appreciation not only on the natural world, but on our responsibility toward it. In White's hands, we come to understand that we should want nothing more than for this life to remain precious."

—**Esteban Rodríguez**, author of *Before the Earth Devours Us* and *Lotería*

"'The end of the exhale is the farthest I find myself willing to venture away from the world,' Lisbeth White writes. 'Then the hunger for the inhale arises, and calmly ravenous, I seek humanity and its company.' In her stunning elemental memoir, *A Most Natural Thing*, Lisbeth's voice is one that 'will never tire of seeing the world, of hearing it everywhere.' Formally inventive, each chapter reflects the elemental force at its core, drawing readers both inward and outward in equal measure—endlessly fascinating, vulnerable, and poignant in its reach. Intimate yet expansive, Lisbeth's work is led by an intelligence that is 'intraterrestrial,' willing to 'follow the dreaming down into the earth, so deep into the earth as to be near the core of creation.' Lisbeth's voice is a prayer—a prayer carried on breath, sometimes a cry, sometimes burning in a moan of pleasure. It's a voice that seeks itself in the heart of hearts—not just the human heart, but its vast extensions—the heart of the whale, the heart of the mountain. This work is alive and searching in its questions of ancestry, grief, love, and, above all, relationship: to ourselves, to each other, to our past, and to the living world in which we are braided. It reminds us that 'we only experience grief to the degree we have experienced love.' We are so fortunate to have this wild little text. It is generous and alive, and its hands are open to bring you inside."

—**Stephanie Adams-Santos,** author of *Dreams of Xibalba*

A Most

Natural

Thing

An Elemental Memoir

Lisbeth White

RED MARE
PRESS

A MOST NATURAL THING

Copyright © Lisbeth White, 2025. A Red Mare Press book.

Published in partnership with *The Masters Review*, an online literary journal.

Edited by Cole Meyer.

Cover design by Emelie Mano.

Interior design by Julianne Johnson.

Cover art by Shreya Delgado-Shah.

RED MARE
PRESS

Red Mare Press / Discover New Art, LLC

70 SW Century Drive, Suite 100442, Bend, Oregon 97702

www.redmarepress.com

Red Mare Press is a division of Discover New Art, LLC.

The Red Mare Press name and logo are trademarks of Discover New Art, LLC.

The publisher is not responsible for websites (or their content) that are not owned by the publisher.

ISBN 979-8-9901838-4-1

Printed in the United States of America.

Always, always, for this earth.

Contents

Acknowledgements

Introduction:
Natural Unnaturalness

If a painter in the nineteenth century could render a mimetic, realistic, three-dimensional picture of a horse, say, on a flat canvas, we would agree even if wasn't art that not everyone could do it. It required skill and training and study and a certain gift, an "eye." The twentieth century arrives along with the cheap Brownie camera and overnight anyone, it seems, can make a picture of a horse. In response, painters, both artists and amateurs, had to face, in the face of such competition, an existential question. What is it that paint can do that a photograph cannot? And they answered with abstraction. Paint as paint. Color for color's sake. Not the illusion of depth but the use of flat-out flat for flat's sake flatness. They answered the challenge by painting what only paint could do.

The same might be said about the nineteenth century narrative writer who took to the field with prose—fiction or nonfiction. What was the competition? Newspapers maybe, another form of narrative delivery device like the novel, like the short story, like the essay. But those forms were printed in newspapers anyway. The twentieth century brings a whole slew of new narrative delivery devices: movies, radio, television, streaming, cable, podcasts, AA meetings. Book writers, writers using print, could respond as the painters did. What is it the book can do, what can print do, that all these other delivery devices cannot do?

A Most Natural Thing: An Elemental Memoir by Lisbeth White is one fine response, a founding example and confounding answer to the question of what only a book can do.

You can't imagine this chapbook as anything other than what it is. What movie could be made of it? It is certainly visual in its making visible the usually invisible conventions and defaults of printing and punctuation. Three columns instead of one! Crots! Dingbats! White spaces! Bullet points! The visual virtuosity here is unique to print and to the defamiliarization of the conventional printed spaces we most often inhabit. And how do you make a podcast or radio report of this *this*? You can't. You can't "follow" it with the ear. It isn't linear. In that sense it doesn't have a "voice." It modulates. It yawns. It barks. There are beautiful types of silences between the buzz of the types of type. It isn't a script. It doesn't have a beginning, middle, or even an end.

You might think of White's memoir more like a map, remembering that like all maps it unfolds and folds. It spreads and bleeds. It is distorted to emphasize and exaggerate. Borges expands that notion, captures the ambitious attempt here when he asks us to imagine a map that is more detailed than the thing it represents. Keep that in mind.

Writers realize that they cannot be abstract in the way that painters can be. I can write **CAT** and you, reader, will think of the four-legged feline, a tracked vehicle, a kind of scan, a house of ill repute. You will not think this: What a lovely sheen in the ink. I like the kern in the spacing. See how the serifs hang and sway. To go abstract Lisbeth White exposes expertly the received gestures found in the acts (already abstract and abstracting) of writing and reading and invites the reader to participate (in new and different ways) in the creation of meaning.

The existential nature of this art form is linear. We read, in English, left to right, word after word, from the top of the page to the bottom. The story wants to line up. Narrative wants to "flow." But *A Most Natural Thing* is unnatural in its great way, and White is adept at the disturbing disruptions on the page, forcing the eye to act differently, to read this narrative the way one "reads" a painting, to see everything all at once. Here is a text that is, yes, elemental. Like fire, earth, water, and air. We are immersed, consumed, engulfed, drowned. Like carbon, *A Most Natural Thing* has four hands. And it places the reader in a printed quantum realm of asymmetrical simultaneity made up of various matrices, lattices, solid and dissolving geometries of texts, sublime and sublimated tetrahedral chains that are fertile, organic, fractured, original.

—**Michael Martone**, guest judge and author of *Plain Air: Sketches from Winesburg, Indiana*; *The Moon Over Wapakoneta*; *Memoranda*; and more

Air

Nine Winds (I am only ever writing about love)

I. *Pandemic*

It is the first week of March when we cross the border into Mexico, continuing the long drive from the temperate rainforest of the Pacific Northwest, and head down the California coast, where the land is roughened into arid boulder. We are now cruising the thin split of the Baja Peninsula, Wayne and I, escaping the heft of Oregon clouds, looking for something as bright and wide open as we wish our hearts to be. We are bumping along roads, lifting dust behind us, driving through plains of saguaros that push up long fingers through brush and white-branched shrubs.

It has been a challenging trip so far. All the ways in which travel surfaces the habits that push us into our separate corners, our ways of trying to anchor stability amongst all the newness. Wayne's body seizes up with the cool Northern Cali temperatures. He gets cold and cranky, finicky about campsites and what he considers to be subpar dining experiences. I roll into my easygoing counterbalance persona, the way I managed the big feelings of the adults around me as a child—everything's fine, whatever you need, I don't have any needs at all. The placid facade behind which I drift further and further away.

There are other challenges we don't yet fully understand. The last news as we hit the border (before the unreliable phone coverage and the infuriatingly slow 3G network), is that this virus with a name vaguely reminiscent of royalty and saints has fully infiltrated both coasts of the United States.

Cases in Washington have spiked the earliest, and while there is still confusion about the levels of danger ("Isn't this just like the flu?"), a fear has been drifting along like a wicked wind behind us all this time. We feel an unease we assign to the other's shitty way of managing travel stress. It is not until we arrive at our rented casita on a hill in the desert between the mountains and the Pacific Ocean, after five days of post-border-crossing travel, that we hear California has issued its first shelter-in-place directive.

Then we see the dust of fear and agitation, how it has gusted along just outside our rolled-up windows. It has been hovering in the air, and even as we quipped two days ago about our lucky timing, we understand now the very act of our breathing has tethered us to the collective gasp of shock at what is happening. There is no escaping air. And that is the thing about pandemics: wherever in the world you go, there they are.

II. *Community spread*

The coronavirus gusting across the globe is actually one of many types of coronaviruses, we learn. By we, I mean those of us who are not scientists and who have not been paying attention. Coronaviruses belong to a group known as single-stranded RNA viruses, apparently notorious for copying errors when they replicate, and for fast evolution. They mutate often, and therefore, evolve quickly. Many scientists believe that if this coronavirus spreads as widely and infects as many people as the seasonal flu, it could kill twenty times as many people.

According to the CDC, symptoms include fever, cough, shortness of breath. Complications include pneumonia, acute respiratory distress syndrome (ARDS), and kidney failure. Risk factors include advanced age and serious underlying medical conditions (e.g. heart disease, diabetes, lung disease, etc.).

These risk factors quickly shift as the virus spreads. At first, the collective story says we are only worried about our elders, folks who already display weakened immune systems, those who belong in what we refer to as "vulnerable populations," which meant who, exactly, in these early days? Maybe people we already deem to be in poor health: those houseless, in active addiction, or constantly surviving chronic illness. But how quickly it shifts, this understanding of who is most vulnerable, as quickly as the virus moves on the air. Because suddenly, we see it is the poor who are rapidly succumbing; those without healthcare coverage who are flooding the emergency rooms; the caretakers and service providers we are all depending on to support us in our quarantines taking the brunt of the exposure risk.

And what constitutes a serious underlying medical condition swiftly demonstrates where we have been failed. Asthma from decades of inhaling the dense air of a populated city after a forced migration, or hypertension and heart disease from the stress of a life under constant threat, or poor nourishment from living in a food desert, or compromised immunity from decades of medical neglect and/or incarceration which keeps you in inescapable quarters of contagion, or lack of access to the lands that nourish you. Nearly every pre-existing condition shows up in a melanated body, a queer body, an impoverished body, a body campaigned openly against as having no worth.

Other than my melanin and my womanness, I am not currently high risk. I understand my low-riskness as the embodiment of several privileges, including access to nature, healthy food, work that is not dependent on an organization that I can do safely from wherever I am. There is a pit gnawing and growing in the place that holds my guts, as I consider how to walk with this privilege of wellness, how to walk with the grace of being in the middle of the desert, Sierras to the east and ocean to the west, and a long broad view of the horizon with few neighbors in sight.

III. *Incubation Period*

This trip was meant to be an adventure deeper into our burgeoning relationship. A first and early adventure, having only been dating about four months. I am as thrilled to settle into the do-nothing moments of being together as I am balking at the awkwardness of having a witness to the amount of hair I sometimes leave in the shower. Though I experience myself as young in many ways, we are both older than any other time we've started relationships and I can feel the difference. Even in that phrasing, "starting a relationship." I did not "start relationships" in my twenties or even thirties; I hung out or hooked up or dated for months or years at a time.

But here we are, on purpose, delving into an unknown in which much will be revealed, and we both know that we can't unknow what we will learn about each other. We're awake to the possibility that this trip might offer up a clarity with no soft edges; that out here in the bright light and broad expanse of desert, with mostly each other to look at, our vision might prove acute. Such acuteness, such willingness and desire to see each other no matter what, is risky. Once we have all the information about our habits, our ways of loving and not loving, we will be in a position to choose. Will we move closer together or distance ourselves across the sandy plain?

The end of our first week in Baja witnesses the closing of all distractions in town. Restaurants, beachside coffee shops, small bars showcasing local musicians, all shut their doors as quarantine and social distancing take hold. It feels like just the two of us scattered on a wind of uncertainty. Though we have chosen this trip, I suddenly feel cast out, so far from home and the familiar. All the habits of self-sufficiency learned in earlier relationships tighten quickly in my chest. I shorten my breath to keep in what I feel makes me vulnerable and weak.

But this isn't how I first learned to breathe. This isn't how I first learned to love, either.

These most natural rhythms are born into our bodies with such ease, we barely feel the separation between them and our own skin. The willingness and desire to see clearly may be a mark of some emotional maturity, but the restriction of breath is a holdover scar from inhaling a toxin or being suffocated by a love too heavy.

I want to know (I want to remember) what it is to be unafraid to love, to be unafraid to breathe.

IV. *Isolation*

They are saying if someone has symptoms, isolation is the socially responsible thing to do. This is before it is "highly suggested," before it becomes a mandate. Before shelter-in-place is a term. Before Black men are forcibly attacked for not wearing masks (a confusing turn after decades of being detained or killed for wearing clothing that was considered to hide guilt). Before white protestors begin swarming city halls with guns and rage to demand access to their barbers. Before the 45th president of the United States announced he would like to open the country up, get the economy going, even though some people will be affected "very badly."

What I hate most about all this is the predictability. Such certain and foreseeable violence. I know what happens to the body in survival mode, real survival mode, like when you are a Black man out for a jog that has suddenly turned into a hunt, being chased down the street by three white men with guns. I know the breath shortens in the body and oxygen fuels systems needed for immediate and urgent use only. I know the rest of the body goes without. I know what atrophies after decades of such deprivation. I have not lost a limb, or a lung, or a brilliant future. But maybe a voice. Maybe a small innocence curled in a corner of my psyche, sipping the smallest bits of air through pursed lips as if buried alive in a cave-in.

Rarefied air. That's what they call those experiences and places of which only the elite get to partake. Something pure. Something nourishing.

Lately, all I can see and think about is care. What must one do to get it? When I was a child, if I took good care of everyone, sometimes they would feel good enough, relaxed enough, nurtured enough, to then shake some of the extra onto me. It wasn't their fault, this shoddy trade. They didn't know they were working from a deficit. We made the best we could with a trickle-down care economy.

Now I know who benefits from such an economy, whose hands were at what tables to create such a system that can deprive and devastate millions. And still, my breath ricochets around in my chest like a pinball. My inhale can't find a pocket to rest.

V. *Shelter in place*

The Baja desert is a long, warm wind from coast to mountain.

It is incredible how much I want to go home.

I don't even know where that really is these days, having been nomadic the past three years. Yet, home preoccupies my thinking. Maybe it is the phrase "shelter-in-place" that makes me want to seek home. Maybe it is just the word shelter and what it means: a structure to provide safety and protection. Maybe it is the notion that such a thing exists. I imagine lying down on earth amidst tall trees and feeling the ground like a grandmother's embrace.

The desert ground is prickly and sharp, only soft in its neutral pastels—sun-softened tans and pale reds. I am surrounded by light and air here, afloat, feeling challenged by the horizon, strangely claustrophobic.

We begin wearing masks into town, and I feel the closeness of my own breath. I feel words reverberate in my mouth as I raise the decibel of my friendliness toward the grocery clerk to translate beyond my face covering. I say, "Thank you!" loudly, with a gratitude in my voice I hope will reach her. I hope she will hear that I mean: "Thank you for being here, because I know you may not have a choice, because I know you being here without a choice is what helps me to be here, and I don't know how to reconcile this." I hope she will hear, "Please, may you be well. Please, may everyone you love be well. Please, understand that I understand you are allowing me to be well." I hope she will hear, "I know there is no thanking you enough."

I hope she will hear that she is loved by me.

This virus travels on air, the single element most necessary for our survival. If we breathe, we die? Where is shelter in this?

In the skin of this new lover, I guess, in the smell of his arms warm from the sun. I am lucky I have someone to touch in this time of forced separation. I am lucky to have someone with whom I can remove the cloth covering from my face, who is willing and able to share the same air. Who will risk putting his cheek near my cheek, rub his thumb across my lower lip and breathe into me. Who opens his mouth against mine so that I can breathe back.

This breath, like a bridge between us.

VI. *Asymptomatic*

Now is when we breathe

.

.

.

.

.

.

.

VII. *Social Distance*

Because the instinct to go home, even when I don't know where that is, lives in my body (my lungs tightening when I think how far away we are), we decide to return to the United States. Because we can. Because we have work that is moveable and a reliable car and blue passports that make us as mobile and free as a glorified wind.

We pass through roadblocks on the way to the border. Thermometers shaped like guns are aimed at our foreheads through car windows. The red pinpoint light checks us for fever, the medical team on the street records our names, date of birth, license plate, destination. We are tracked like the migrating animals we are.

My friends from Northern California send me links to photos of coyotes wandering the near-empty streets of San Francisco. An article pops up about a brown bear venturing into a city in Northern Spain that, while part of its original territory, hasn't been visited by this bear in 150 years. My friend, Tiffany, in the Bay tells me she is marveling at how loud the birds seem to be this spring. With all the human activity hushed and indoors, other sounds rise above our din. Or, with us contained, there is space enough on the earth for all beings to roam.

I think about this as we curve up the San Jacinto mountains, Avii Hanupach in Mojave, a mountain range east of Los Angeles that peaks in elevation at 10,834 feet. I think about what it means that we can go here, to this place where the air might be clearer, where trees outnumber people, where I can sit at the base of a towering Western Red Cedar in the morning and gaze up at its flat green fronds waving kindly in the breeze.

I think about this as we stop in the nearly deserted central square of the small town where we will be self-quarantining for the next several weeks. I think about this as I hop out of the car to stretch my legs after the long drive, without a mask on, my lungs loosening. I think about this as a very large and very white man, a mountain local standing outside his own car about twenty feet away, begins to scream at me.

"I don't want to catch whatever the fuck you have! Put a fucking mask on! Goddamn flatlanders."

He is screaming at me because he is scared. He is screaming at me because I am black-brown and woman and the easiest body that he can police. He is screaming at me because I will come and I will go, and he has been here, and he will stay.

I think about how, after all these centuries of practice, we struggle still to share the space of the world. We struggle still to be free, and together.

VIII. *Flattening the curve*

Someone calls the pandemic a portal. Someone says this is a time we can do something different than what we have done before. Someone believes maybe we can take what has been failing the majority of us and create systems that heal.

Madagascar finds an herbal remedy to support the health of its citizens, which was distributed for free to the most vulnerable populations. New Zealand contains the virus completely within five weeks by adhering to strict standards of quarantining that limited access to public spaces and closed business. In Ireland, descendants of the Great Famine donate more than half a million dollars to support the Navajo and Hopi nations being ravaged by the virus. This is an offering in remembrance of a solidarity from more than 150 years ago, when the Choctaw peoples raised money to send to Ireland for those suffering hunger.

It is true, at times, I read this news and it feels like hope, which feels something like love.

Far away but happening. I don't know if this makes me feel more or less alone. The world is turning, and I am here, in a holding, holding and being held, being held and being held in.

As someone who takes pride in a capacity for solitude and stillness, I am surprised when tears spring because I find myself missing the world. I am missing the world of simple exchanges and gestures, the world of slight kindnesses and communion. The world where we head-nod to each other on the street and see each other's smiles breaking across our faces like wild horses.

When I go to my altar in the mornings, I sit and breathe and try for the longest exhale, the biggest inhale. I am able to get to an exhale count of eight, then a beat, followed by an inhale count of six. About fifteen slow seconds, and at the bottom of the exhale is a stillness that feels dark and soft as the cosmos.

The end of the exhale is the farthest I find myself willing to venture away from the world. Then the hunger for inhale arises, and calmly ravenous, I seek humanity and its company.

IX. *Herd Immunity*

By week seven of sheltering in place, my sister, my cousin, and I have coordinated the time we spend at our altars. We sit together, our altars distant from each other by thousands of miles, and think about the world breathing between us.

By week seven of sheltering in place, Wayne and I are calling each other partner. We will never know what our relationship might have been without this time bestowed upon us by a virus. Time like a faulty gift, splintered with grief and fear, limiting contact outside our small circle of two, but we would never return it. To return this faulty gift slings us into a set of questions neither of us is truly prepared for or wanting. And anyway, return to who? The gods of plague have already taken so much.

By week ten of sheltering in place, most states will begin "opening up," language that brings the image of strip mall doors flinging as wide as we hope the arms of our loved ones will open to us. It is still not clear who we will see, who we will touch, who we will sit close to for a meal.

Wayne and I will begin our drive north up the coast at week eleven, heading in the opposite direction as when we started out, toward a place we imagine we will call home for some time. On the way, we will pass my family's house, where my mom is taking care of my 97-year-old grandparents, but I don't know if we will stop to visit. I don't know if it is safe enough for me to see my grandparents alive again.

In the meantime, I am writing this on the deck of the mountain cabin we have been staying in these past weeks. The sun is moving near its golden hour and the evening stretches close to summer. The breeze is warm and dry, constant, like it has been moving in this direction a long time coming.

I am remembering lines of a Merwin poem I heard read aloud through a computer screen just a few days before:

"Listen/ with the night falling we are saying thank you…" it begins. "we are saying thank you and waving/ dark though it is," it ends.

I know I am one of those who will do this: turn a face of grateful tears towards a god who seems to have not shown mercy, perhaps for years. Not because I love an abuser, but because even the insects with their gaggle of legs and waspy wings move into a pocket of evening light above me and can look like fairies, wicked and delicate. I will never tire of seeing this world, of hearing it everywhere, the tight whimper or sigh or howl from a hospital or from behind a mask or in a deserted central square. I am so grateful for a noise as animal and human and gashing and gorgeous as I know we can be when we are all the way alive.

This terror of being. Those of us who live.

We live.

Some of us, we live.

Fire

Shed

During the ceremony, I am asked
to tend fire. This is a duty I like
to hold: I get to be outside in
the cool breath of night and stars
while the raucousness of healing
happens on the other side of the
sliding glass doors. I hear the
singing, drumming, the sometimes wail of a release. Here,
I've been taught to tend to fire
as an ancestor. The same way my
freshman biology teacher asked
us if fire was a living thing and, if
so, to prove it. It's alive, half of us
said. It consumes, it reproduces,
it dies and leaves something
behind (even if that something
is devastation). It is a different
fire every time. I see this as I am
focused on keeping this particular
fire alive for the duration of
the ceremony. Unlike the fire
yesterday, this one wants more
air, less wood. It is responding to
the stillness around me, the winds
having calmed with the sunset.
I am paying attention as it leaps
and ebbs, watching the flames
like a language, like the flickering
tongue of a snake.

I want to write this in a language
of fire. Which takes a surprising
amount of patience. Like fire
tending. Not all fast-burn and
heat and destruction and rage.
Though all I can feel now is
urgency, resistance, fight. The
desire. The truth that, even as I
write this, it will change more
quickly than I can anticipate. The
reader's gaze will shift and in that
split between the words and the
reader's attention, whatever story
there is will shapeshift. Become
a different fire than the one we
started with. Yes, still fire. But
transformed by its needs now to
something else. And its needs in
this moment, transforming once
again. Alive, alive, and changing.
Never the same fire twice. Yet all
the same fire at once.

My friend Tiffany (fiery Aries)
and I somehow end up in a
Google rabbithole researching the
Vestal Virgins. The Vestal Virgins
were women who lived in a
temple dedicated to guarding and
feeding fires considered sacred
to the times. The Eternal Flame,
they say. Guarding and feeding
and anticipating needs. One site
describes the Vestal Virgins as suffering in chastity, those women
who were punished and sent to
live in a temple to guard fires to
be used for religious purposes or
war. They underwent terrible,
degrading initiations and were
not allowed to look pretty.

Occasionally, someone from
inside, wiped and trembling from
medicine, will be brought out
to bask in the warmth of what
I've tended.

I want to write this in the shape
of a snake. Slithering and winding. A story swallowed whole
and pushed, rib by rib, through
the body. To the gut. Not
dismembered but a disintegrating
palimpsest. Each layer emerging
from the shadow of the last.
Skin-shed like ash. The tail end
entering my mouth as I open it
to speak the beginning. Like the
ouroboros. The beginning and
the end at once.

One especially bright autumn,
I saw twenty-three small snakes
over the course of my hike,
sunning themselves on the trail.
Late October, after my grandfather died. Getting the last of
the fall warmth and whipping
away into the shadows upon
my heavy-footed approach. I
remember wondering, what if
I walked more lightly? What if
I also slithered, my own body
winding flexible and lithe, one
long muscle of belly on the earth?
Would they stay in their basking,
let me join them and we could
seep the sun's warmth into

Vesta, the Roman goddess of the
hearth, is also the name of an
asteroid. A ball of fire streaking
through the cosmos. This fact
delights me.

There seems to be a patriarchal
hierarchy to research. A slow re-
veal of information for the seeker
with stamina. A search engine
layer deeper, Tiffany and I come
across the independence afforded
to the Vestal Virgins. *Virgin* here
is used to mean a woman who
belongs to no man. Living in the
temple as a guardian of the flame
meant these were women who
did not marry and who no longer
lived in their father's home, thus
they were not the "property"
of any man. *Virgin* meaning a
woman who belongs to her Self
and whatever duty she decides is
sacred to her.

the hot core of ourselves, the
pleasure seeping out, a coven
of skin-shedders?

One busy spring, in love with a
young man, I stumbled across
a lazily half-hidden DVD—or
maybe it was a web browser left
almost casually open—and there
was a woman or two, shaved and
splayed like a sheep shorn for
slaughter, assholes and pussies raw
red and swollen from a pounding,
mouths open in a violent parody
of pleasure, grotesque, distorted,
static somehow. Try as I might with
my sex-positive politics, an electric
burn seared from stomach to my
fingertips. It's not me he was watching, imagining in this way, but
wasn't it? Wasn't this woman-as-

One sunny morning, making love
with Wayne with house guests
in the next room, I held in the
wailing type of moan that cracks
from my throat while cumming.
I swallowed it at the moment
of orgasm and I felt it move out
through my skin, a tingly surge
from the inside layer, the delicate
mycelia of nerves crisscrossing between muscle and dermis alight.
Then one giant pulse out through
my pores, the air humming, my
skin shivering right off.

One night after a bonfire, I
dreamt myself in an old-timey
European village, and an old
Italian witch spread my skirted
legs and chanted between them.
I saw magical symbols floating
like embers from her mouth to
land on my vaginal walls, now
decorated with glyphs like the
paintings of cave dwellers or
the tombs of Egyptian royals.
Something ancient recorded
there, is what I mean. Something
sacred. Something magic.

Digging deeper, we get to the
really good stuff. The embers.
The association of the Vestal
Virgins to sacred prostitution.
If the designation *virgin* simply
means a woman who belongs to
no one but herself, it has nothing
to do with being sexually chaste
or celibate. In fact, in the time
of Goddess worship, the Vestal
Virgins were said to take many
lovers, that this was part of

penile-punching-bag, woman-as-soft-flesh-begging-to-be-ripped, woman-as-lascivious recipient-of-objectification—wasn't this projected on my ass like a screen as I was on my knees quivering before him?

One frigid winter evening, seeking heat, I met a man, older than me, who fucked me like a porn star. Which is to say, he fucked me like fucking him was my job, not an offering. Like I was on his payroll and owed him everything he wanted. He could not be bothered to worry about my Self, and I was too young to believe that mattered in the face of his desire. Where would I have found such information telling me anything different? He fucked his rage, his disdain, into me without a condom and two days later blisters like bee stings erupted at the tender opening of my vagina.

One humid lazy late afternoon, laying on my bed masturbating, I found myself spending a little more time on the right side of my clitoris than I normally do. I was experiencing sensations that felt somewhat familiar but in some ways completely unknown. There was pleasure to be sure, but I had no idea if it would get me anywhere (and by that I of course mean to orgasm). Still I lingered, becoming fascinated really because it dawned on me I had no idea what was going to happen. It felt good, and I suddenly had the thought that I could do this forever. I could breathe and feel good, for as long as I cared to do so. It struck me as such liberation, suddenly so simple a freedom to gain. To breathe and feel good for as long as I cared. Is this privilege? I thought. Is this sovereignty? Is this radical joy? Am I free?

tending to the Sacred Flame, which represented life force energy and the cycle of creation/destruction/creation or birth/death/rebirth.

Tiffany and I theorize that this reproductive sexual ceremony was actually the heart, the core, of what was represented by the sacred fires. Juiced up by this theory, it isn't a stretch for us to get very quickly to an understanding that sacred prostitution was not about satisfying men in a sexual way. That, in fact, it was probably not male-centered at all. We imagine that men would come to offer their life force (semen) to the Vestal Virgins as tithe or service to the Divine Feminine. Tithe to the goddess. Tithe to be in the presence of the goddess. So these virgins were, in reality, priestesses. Guardians of transformation, whose first gateway is pleasure.

What a delight I was. I am. Never the same fire twice.

Some months, if I eat too much sugar, or feel too much anger, or shame, or weakness in myself, or someone looks or speaks to me like I am not a human but a bother or a grossness or a receptacle for whatever waste or fantasy they would like to run out of themselves and into my body, the skin around the softness of my genitals flares up an angry, shameful rash and I must fight the reminder of the violence that dehumanized me, the violent dehumanizing of me, the me violently dehumanized.

Is this, too, a kind of sex magic? The Self gone, now the Fantasy Fuck Avatar. Perhaps, a dark sorcery.

Why does it seem we don't know how to tend anymore? To each other. To anything. Why can't we seem to look, to listen, until we see, really see, what might be required or helpful or interesting to grow, for something new to happen, for something we can't completely control but something we can help to create?

Life-force energy, sometimes called Ka. Sometimes called kundalini and known to move from the base of the spine up the body like a snake.

Moving from the Vestal Virgins
to Mary Magdalene, we find
there is some study that she was a
priestess of Isis, and thus trained
in the sexual alchemies that
open the conduits of life force
energy. There is some study that
these tantric practices prepared
Jesus for his resurrection. As Isis
remembered Osiris after his death
and back into life. Breathing
up the fire that is the life-spark,
passing through her lips, through
her vagina, into his body, resur-
rected. Sex magic.

Mary Magdalene in her tantra,
building up and strengthening
the Ka body, which is already
luminous, radiates more light. We
recognize, we have the potential
to recognize, to have an experience of the Self, to see and open
and bask in the Self of the other.

Why are we so scared to open a space that might be bigger than what we can imagine? Why are we so scared to become a light of possibility?

I want to write this into the shape of a snake. Slithering and winding. A story swallowed whole and pushed, rib by rib, through the body. To the gut. Not dismembered but a disintegrating palimpsest. Each layer emerging from the shadow of the last. Skin-shed like ash. The tail-end entering my mouth as I open it to speak the beginning. Like the ouroboros. The beginning and the end at once.

Like fire tending. Not all fast-burn and heat. The Desire gets us there. And then the story will change more quickly than we can anticipate. Become a different fire than the one we started with. Yes, still fire. But transformed by what it needs now to something else. Alive, alive, and changing.

One easy sunset, Wayne traces the world between my legs with fingertips so slowly, so passionately, so tenderly, I thought, "Something is being called forth." I thought, "A temple is opening." I thought, "There is a being of astonishing power and presence and pleasure in there." I thought, "We could make anything happen." I thought: "Magic."

Like the sun's own rays. The
flame of Self is this precious. In
this illuminated space, fantasy,
while wonderful for its generative
spark, quickly burns through the
limits of its predictability. What
we have cultivated as our desire
pales in the luminosity of a truly
creative field. We don't know
what may happen here. We must
surrender to the newness of what
can now be created.

While sitting in ceremony, the
candlelight to the left of the
altar kept flickering. Flickering.
Catching my attention from the
periphery like a flare. Distracted,
I let my gaze be pulled from the
center prayer into the center-blue
of a flame. Fixed there. My
focus so focused. Stillness in
the center of me. Then, it felt
like my hips cracked open and
suddenly snakes, snakes, snakes
everywhere—slipping

Sitting outside that morning after
ceremony, the pine trees swaying
and my arms bare to the sun,
there is a moment when I understand that the warmth is felt only
because I am there, conscious of
it on my own skin, present to its
light and its touch. I have agreed
to be awake to it, to let it exist
with me, to let myself exist with
it. I have agreed to meet the Sun's
Self with my open awakeness, my
Self. To meet this Celestial being
with my human being. And the
whole world lights up.

Yes.
I want to be my Self.
I want to be this
precious.

through my hip sockets like oil,
coiling down my thighs, winding
up over my belly. I could hear
the hissing like a roar of whispers
through my ears, joints, back of
my skull. Hissing like a memory
or prayer or instruction. Hissing
like a code. And the facilitator
holding the ceremony asks me to
go out for the next round. Asks
me to tend the fire.

Water

A Discipline of Kindness

There are no monologues in the sea.
— *Charles Foster*

The sea is history.
— *Derek Walcott*

To destroy the sovereignty of a people, you must first destroy their name.
— *common knowledge*

- I am at the end of the world and I am praying for whales.
- Only it's not the end of the world, it is just nearing the end of summer.
- Only it's not the end of the world, just the westernmost point of the contiguous United States, Cape Flattery at the tip of Washington State, where my phone thinks I am in Canada, though really, I am on Makah land. I have been living all summer on the Olympic Peninsula, near Indianola, whose true name is not Indianola.
- I am at the end of Washington State where the Pacific Ocean, listing endlessly from the western horizon, carries its water through this entrance to Puget Sound.
- In nearly every earth-based healing tradition, water is known as a "clear soul liquid." Meaning, it is a conduit of high vibrational quality.

Meaning, it is a pure channel through which information from spiritual realms can sing.

- I am praying for whales because I fear I have lost poetry. Meaning, I
  miss my auntie, the one who was a poet, the one who taught me to
  turn my daydreams into poems, the one who lived on a cove above
  the Pacific Ocean filled with kelp beds where humpback whales
  would come to feed their calves. Every time they swam near, my
  auntie would say they were coming to visit with me, lonely child
  that I was. As if I were known.

- Grief is a threshold emotion. Meaning, it is an emotion that is
  actually an altered state of being. Loss wrenches the ground from
  underneath us. We free float and are tossed through waves of rage,
  sorrow, betrayal, pain. We may walk through our days as if we are
  simple bodies walking through our days. In truth, we are adrift on
  a body much bigger.

- S'Klallam, Suquamish, Swinomish. The land I have been on
  all summer.

- Last week I watched the Indigenous peoples of the Pacific Northwest
  coast gather for the intertribal canoe journeys throughout the Puget
  Sound, some coming from as far as southeast Alaska. The canoes,
  holding families, paddle for miles and weeks, asking for permission
  from the community whose home they are visiting before they dis-
  embark on each bank.

- This permission asked, this discipline of kindness, opens a fissure
  the front length of my body. I can feel my insides spilling along the
  boating docks as they wait to be granted the gift of visiting a place
  another calls home—this title that makes any place sacred.

~

- Humpback whales are the most frequently seen visitors in the Puget
  Sound. Humpback whales grow to be about fifty-two feet, weigh

thirty to fifty tons and have a four-chambered heart that weighs about 430 pounds.

- The weight of a humpback whale's heart is about as much as the weight of three average adult human beings.

- I am praying for whales because I fear I have lost poetry. Meaning all summer, Black trans women and Indigenous women have been disappeared with casualness. We learn their names only after they are found dead. Then we add it to the numbers.

- A canoe lands on the shores of the Suquamish reservation and all the women inside have red handprints painted over their mouths, in protest, in remembrance of the disappeared.

- How do we call to those who are refused a name? How do we sing to them? How do we say they are known?

- An Igbo proverb says when a person is given a name, the spirit accepts it. Your name has celestial powers and embodies that spirit.

- Two weeks before I am standing on the westernmost tip of the contiguous United States, the Pacific Ocean endless on the horizon, Seattle's waste management system leaks about three million gallons of untreated sewage into the Puget Sound after a failure at the West Point Treatment Plant. For a half hour, sewage is spilled into the water near North Beach in Discovery Park.

- The Suquamish Tribe are known as "The People of the Clear Salt Water."

- The naming ceremonies of Yorubaland, which is part of West Africa, is much more than deciding what to call a child. It is a process of determining the entire destiny of that child, since it is believed that a child eventually lives out the meaning of their name.

- My name, Lisbeth, is a variation of Elizabeth, which means "close to God."

- In the naming ceremonies of Yorubaland, an elder presides over the event with seven symbolic items that are traditionally used to express hope or the path of a successful life. The first symbolic item that the elder presents to the child is water.

- Water is everlasting and has no enemies since everything in life needs water to survive. Meaning, the child will never be thirsty in life and no enemy will slow their growth.

- Humpback whales are the noisiest and most imaginative whales when it comes to songs. They have long, varied, complex, eerie and beautiful songs that include recognizable squeaks, grunts, and other sounds. The songs have the largest range of frequencies used by whales, ranging from 20-90,000 hertz.

- Sound travels four and a half times faster in water than it does in air.

- My mother's middle name is Elizabeth, with a z. My sister's middle name is Elisabeth, with an s.

- It is my auntie who teaches me to pour libation. Forms of pouring libation vary widely, but they are intended to acknowledge the contributions and continued spiritual presence of our ancestors. She shows me how to fill a glass with water, then speak into it what we are grateful for, what we hope for the world. I am shy so I whisper into my glass. Then we go outside to the big cedar tree and kneel at the base. She says to call out the name of each person in my family that I remember and to pour a bit of the water into the earth after each one. We call the names of our family members who have passed and those of revered ancestors.

- Even if we don't know their names, she says, we call them relatives and pour.

- One famous Japanese researcher and author believed that water can react to positive and negative words or thoughts, and if water is polluted, then it can be cleansed through prayers and positive imagination.

~

- As a teenager, I enacted a small but pointed rebellion by changing the spelling of my name from Lizbeth with a z to Lisbeth with an s. Was I trying to hide my true name? Be less like my mother?

Closer to my sister? I couldn't completely divorce myself from the letters tying me to the women of my family. Or maybe, already feeling a vague world of grief in my body, already dreaming of memories not mine, already hoping to somehow be known, I couldn't completely divorce myself from the way my name kept me close to God.

- In cold waters, humpback whales make rough sounds, scrapes and groans, perhaps used for locating large masses of krill. In warm waters, they sing complex songs.

- Two summers before the summer I am praying for whales, I am in a ceremony on the islands of South Carolina, home to the Gullah/Geechee for many hundred years. In the ceremony, I am surrounded by Black women, priestesses, and healers. They are pouring water over me. The water has been soaked with flowers and herbs. While they pour the water, they are whispering, speaking, chanting words of blessing. The water mixes with tenderness and my tears. One of the women, Aset, whispers a blessing and smiles. Her cheekbones look like my grandmother's.

- My last name, White, comes from my father's side. His father and his father's people are Black South Carolinians since the beginning of South Carolina. The name White is most certainly the name of the plantation owner, given to those enslaved on the land.

- I am praying for whales because I fear I have lost poetry. Meaning, I am faltering in my tolerance of grief, how long the arc of it stretches across time.

- After the ceremony, Aset finds me. We chat and smile, and, noticing each other's cheekbones, ask, "Where are your people from?"

- Aset has taken a Kemetic name. Aset's surname at birth was also White.

- Grief is a threshold emotion. Meaning, it is an emotion that carries its own opposite within it. We only experience loss to the degree we experience connection to what we have lost. We only experience the death or passing away of a thing to the degree we have felt its vitality within and vitalness to us. We only experience grief to the degree we have experienced love.

- Among the Northern Soho-, Southern Soho-, and Batswana-speaking people in South Africa, a person's name held immense spiritual power. So much so that it was extremely important to conceal your true name until tremendous trust was built between yourself and another. Only then would your true name be revealed.
- S'Klallam, Suquamish, Swinomish. My tongue spills the names.

~

- I am praying for whales because I fear I have lost poetry. Meaning, I fear I have lost the language that can make beauty out of loss, love out of suffering, reverence out of grief.
- It is believed every molecule in water reacts towards the surrounding situation. Therefore, water transmits the information and keeps the memory. A study observed that, when different flowers were dipped in different water jars, every molecule in the droplet of water contained the shape of the flower that was dipped into it.
- In June of the summer that I am praying for whales, the Suquamish Tribe announces its intention to sue the US Navy for repeatedly releasing raw sewage into the Puget Sound. According to public records, the Navy discharged hundreds of thousands of gallons of untreated sewage from the Naval Base Kitsap in repeated incidents over the past five years. Some of these spills continued unchecked for weeks, even months. One lasted for more than four years.
- Every culture in the world has a ritual for water.
- Only the heart the size of a whale can hold grief the size of humanity.
- One week before I am standing on the westernmost tip of the contiguous United States, the Pacific Ocean endless on the horizon, praying for a heart the size of a whale's heart, I have a dream. In the dream, the whales in Puget Sound are suffocating in the waters. In the dream, a woman tells me to bring a jar of water to where the

ocean enters the Sound. She tells me to pray into it and make it an offering. But, she says, the water in the jar must be sweet waters, must be freshwater. First, I must go to a mountain waterfall, a very specific one, and ask if I can bring water from the falls to help the waters in the Sound. If the waterfall says yes, I am to collect the fresh mountain waters, sing a blessing into them, and offer them to the entrance of the Sound.

- I am to ask permission.
- Rocky Brook Falls is on the southeastern edge of the Olympic National Forest, outside of Quilcene, Washington. The waters cascade over 229 feet of a wide wall of dark rock, and there are boulders holding a large green pool at its base. In some places, the water launches off a jutting edge of stone and seems to suspend for a moment in its fall, the way a diver appears to hover for just a split second before the plunge. In some places, the rock slopes with moss and fern, and the water slips gently down amongst them.
- Named Rocky Brook Falls for over one hundred years, though no one knows where the name came from.

~

- If you listen deep enough, everything has a sound. If you learn to hear it, you'll be surrounded by memory. If you learn to name what you hear, you'll be surrounded by relatives.
- My ancestors were stacked in the belly of, not a whale, but a monster of tremendous appetite that ate up the seas. We know that thousands of them were tossed into the waters like so much bad waste. Babies, sisters, fathers. We know the lore of the Igbo, who landed on shore, and turning in their chains, walked back into the sea before they could be called anything other than themselves.
- I am alone at Rocky Brook Falls for about twenty minutes, rare for this popular summer swimming hole. While I am alone, I roll up my pant legs and wade into the pool toward the falling water. It is

cool and clear. I slip my hand through the waterfall to touch the face of the rock, which is also cool. I mean to ask for permission to collect water but suddenly my heart is aching, and what I find myself asking for is the waterfall's true name. Then I am crying.

- My auntie died the summer after I graduated from high school. I have her name written on a piece of paper I keep under a glass bowl filled with water on my writing desk.

- Grief is a threshold emotion. Meaning, it is an entrance. Meaning, if you give it permission to land in your heart, it will take you to the truest name of your grief and tell you how to make an offering of it. It will teach you the honor of right address. Which is poetry.

Earth

Sanctuary: Rock: Mountain: Home

▲▲▲▲

The summer of 2018 I ran away to the mountains, living at the base of the Pisgahs, a part of the Blue Ridge mountain range in North Carolina.

My running away was not a big deal in the scheme of big deals or even in the scheme of running away. Running this way was just a pattern of discomfort; perhaps post-breakup, but more likely a rupture of the edging loneliness beneath the surface of my well-polished independence. Loneliness shifting under my life like tectonic plates. I felt the ground begin to rumble and grabbed the go-bag.

I don't know if this type of lonely rupture happens more often to me than other people, but it certainly feels like more. It feels like a wish for safety I have had my whole life. I was a soft, dreamy child and I still want to love the world that way, to feel like it is safe to love the world in such a way—with heart and hands wide open.

I came to those mountains because I believed they are sacred. This is kind of a lie.
Not that I believe mountains are sacred, but that I believed the Blue Ridge to be mountains.

After three months of living in Asheville, I hadn't been able to call them mountains yet. They didn't look like mountains to me but simply large furry hills. Their rounded summits weren't daunting against the sky, no sheer faces taunted climbers. I learned this arrogance from the mountains of the Pacific Northwest, young mountains that thrust up showy in their new crags, dramatized by shadows of snow and crevice. Those were not humble mountains but apexes bold in their majesty, requiring an equally bold character of those who wanted to ascend their peaks. I had not acquired that brand of boldness, but I still felt comfortable snubbing the Pisgahs, and in fact the whole range of the Appalachians, by denying them this title.

I was lonely, having moved to town knowing no one and nothing but my own desire to get to mountains, mountains, mountains, after a summer in Brooklyn.

More than that, I had been traveling for eight months straight.
More than that, I had been praying to feel home.

▲▲▲▲

I think of the Mary Oliver line often: "Tell me about despair, yours, and I will tell you mine/ Meanwhile, the world goes on."

I want to say it another way: "Tell me about your home and I will tell you about mine…"

I wonder how many people know their homes.
I wonder how many people know their homes without longing or separation.
I wonder how many of us feel home without a sense of grief. Or if that is part of what makes home.

I wonder if what makes home is a leaving and rediscovering of it; the destruction and the recreation of it over time.

I left home when I was seventeen, just for a time, and lived in the mountains of south-central Mexico with a tenuous amount of Spanish and a host family that didn't speak English. I was alone, marooned with the mountains and the small town of crumbling adobe. Until I wasn't. A group of friendly teenagers enfolded me and, six months later, I cried to leave the new world I had let be made around me.

I came back to the town I grew up in, which I *thought* was my home, and felt how much it hated me, hated my brown skin against the gray cloud cover, under the white gaze.

Meanwhile, the world goes on.

▲▲▲▲

My grandfather holds my first memory of mountain.

He was not mountainous to look at. He was slim and wiry through the forest. I once wrote a poem about him walking the woods "loose-hipped, legs swinging like a whip."

Tatoosh Peak was my first summit, a summer I was nine and, being so young, much of my gear was distributed through the packs of three adults. This left me light-footed enough to clip the heels of my grandfather leading us through high alpine meadows with slopes so green and so vibrant, it hurt the eyes under full sun. We walked as many deer trails as human hiking trails. Deer trails marked only by a crushed leaf or one bent blade of grass, delicate and subtle, as if walking a mountain was a refined act. As if the tread should reflect such reverence.

We slept without tents on a ridge that bottomed out to a lake, still aqua blue from ice. We had passed a wolverine that afternoon but no one seemed worried about that.

The stars were many, so many beyond how we had learned to talk about them, that we didn't. We stayed quiet and awake much of the night, sleeping bags pressed together beneath a sky glistening as glitter, trying to keep our eyes open.

Trying to capture all the light we could.

▲▲▲▲

Fewer than three miles from where I now live is a huge stone, an ancient monolith protected by the Jamestown S'Klallam tribe, called the Tamanowas Rock Sanctuary. There are two gates into the trailheads: two beautiful wooden fences, both formed by L-shapes coming towards each other so that you enter on the right, turn to the left and then exit onto a heavily forested path. The effect is a brief moment in which you are between two cedar walls, a moment which feels long and still even though you are walking. A moment that feels deeply private before the path presents itself before you.

This is a threshold.

The interpretive brochure informs that Tamanowas Rock was formed before the surrounding Cascade Mountains range. It is older than those mountains.

Tamanowas Rock is forty-three million years old.

I press my ear against its eastern side, the side green with moss and ferns where squirrels with short tails are chirping their scattering announcement of my arrival. When I find its cool rough surface and lean my body against it, I can hear that Tamanowas Rock is forty-three million years old. I can hear its forty-three-million-year-old heart, a low rumble forty or fifty feet in towards its center. A rumble like far thunder or the beginning turn of a volcano, something simultaneously immense and intimate. The surface of the earth will change from this place, but first, a sound like a deep belly hum, almost a lullaby, a sound like a cradle, rocking us along.

▲▲▲▲

Meanwhile, the summer of 2018, living at the base of the Pisgahs, I started making sure to fill up my gas tank only while in town, having stopped two or three times at a country sideroad station alongside a large truck with a confederate flag decal on the rear window and a MAGA sticker on the bumper.

Glad for self-service, I filled my tank quickly, suddenly damp and sticky beside the pump, not knowing when the vehicle owners would come out of the convenience mart, not knowing if they were southerners who valued politeness over an opportunity to flex power. I only knew that if the conditions weren't just right, there would be little they'd suffer in the way of consequence should they deem my black-brown woman body as inflammatory and choose to dispose of it in any way they saw fit.

I circumambulated this knowing nearly every time I have left the house since the age of twelve. This knowing circumambulated me even before then, when drunk men would stumble onto our front porch, and my single mother, there with her two daughters, would joke and laugh them gently down the front steps of our home.

Meanwhile, the summer of 2018, I remember this knowing again as news begins to surface of "tender-age camps" at the southern border of the U.S. Images of children behind wire fencing, six-year-olds taking care of two-year-olds. Rumors, then proof, of sexual abuse by armed guards. Parents by the hundreds trucked miles away.

▲▲▲▲

Mountains are threshold places: earth as it appears closest to the heavens and landscape best suited for those who can live liminally, between worlds.

There is Mount Taranaki, sacred in Maori mythology as a site where life is given and where people are returned after death.

Tibet's Mount Kailash is a sacred place to five religions: Buddhism, Jainism, Hinduism, Bon Po (a native Tibetan religion prior to Buddhism), and Ayyavazhi religions. According to some Hindu tradition, Mount Kailash is the home of the deity Shiva.

According to the Torah, and consequently the Old Testament of the Bible, Mount Sinai is the location where Moses received the Ten Commandments directly from God.

Mount Meru is a cosmic mountain which is described to be one of the highest points on Earth and is the center of all creation. Folklore suggests the mountain rose from the ground piercing the heavens, giving it the moniker, "navel of the universe."

These mountains are associated with the masculine god, but doesn't that phrase, "navel of the universe," make you think of an umbilical cord? Doesn't it make you think of your own belly button, puckered tight after the separation from your mother?

▲▲▲▲

I grew up in a land of mountains and water. Water from the sky and criss-crossing rivers, the mountains held the strongest points on the horizon, containing the valley.

The places I grew up in the Pacific Northwest felt seeping, water-logged, with edges and boundaries that slid and suctioned with the heft of mud. These are adjectives that could be used just as easily to describe the dynamics of my family. Not harsh, but with so much leaching out, so much being sucked under, it was not necessarily safe either.

I once wrote a poem about my maternal grandmother and my mother. I wrote about them and the sea. The wild sea, the tempestuous sea. The sea aghast and suddenly violent with its own power; the motherhood that tosses the smallest bodies about the waves.

I am also a woman of water, a woman fascinated with how light fractals into depths, a woman constantly dancing the line between anchor and buoyancy.

Do I seek the mountains for a different kind of holding, something more solid and firm?

There is an intelligence mandated by existing in the mountains. Some believe the mountains to be a place of extraterrestrial intelligence, but I think it must be intraterrestrial. One must be willing to follow their dreaming down into the earth, so deep into the earth as to be near the core of creation, from which everything we touch and see is generated. Into the earth to gather from source the raw material our dreaming wants to touch and be held by.

Origin.

▲▲▲▲

Tamanowas Rock Sanctuary was an ancient sanctuary for hunting and ceremony before humans newer to the area decided to utilize it as a bouldering site. Then, covered with graffiti, it was fought to be reclaimed by the Jamestown S'Klallam peoples. It was then sold to the Jefferson County Land Trust, who offered to be a bridge loan to the Jamestown S'Klallam tribe until they could buy it back from public use to become a sanctuary once more.

Having been witness to the spiritual tourism and New-Age desecration of Mount Shasta (mystics excavating stones from the mountainside, self-proclaimed shamans depositing crystals and ash at the springs of sacred origin from which the Winnemem Wintu peoples bubbled forth), the Jamestown S'Klallam tribe issued a code of conduct for visitors to Tamanowas Rock.

There is a clear list designating what activities are appropriate for visitors who are not members of the Jamestown S'Klallam tribe. There are times of year the Tamanowas Rock Sanctuary is not open to the public. There are protocols for sitting in passive reverence. The way one might sit in attendance at the church of a close friend of a different faith but who has invited you in anyway. Because there is prayer enough to share.

▲▲▲▲

Meanwhile, that June of 2018, the Trump administration established a new policy of separating parents from their children at the Mexican border. Later investigations found that the practice of family separations had begun a year prior to the public announcement. People asking for asylum at official ports of entry were being turned away and told there's no room for them.

That June of 2018, US Attorney General Jeff Sessions disqualified victims of gangs or domestic violence to be reasonable causes for seeking asylum.

By the end of the summer of 2018, the Trump administration announced new rules to deny asylum to anyone who crossed into the United States illegally from any nation, at Trump's discretion. Trump signed a proclamation to specify that people crossing the Mexican border illegally would not qualify for asylum; he called the march of migrants from Central America towards the United States a "crisis."

He did not mean a crisis for those seeking asylum. He meant a crisis for those of us being asked to share our safety.

▲▲▲▲

What does it mean to cross a mountain?

Some religions circumambulate them—make the circular treks as pilgrimage, winding and unwinding in the medicine of walking, dreaming mountain dreams, each step asking for a vision or a nirvana.

Is crossing a mountain the same as crossing a border? Is crossing a border the same as pilgrimage?

▲▲▲▲

It is said the mountains give special dreams, medicine dreams, that should be noted and taken seriously.

A scientist may relate this type of intense dreaming to altitude sickness. When the body is exposed to low amounts of oxygen at high elevation, it can experience nausea, swelling, headaches, fatigue, dizziness, insomnia, loss of appetite, and (to my dark delight) "pins and needles sensation."

I relate this dreaming to the presence of beings powerful enough to have learned to survive in such places, places of thin oxygen and drastic temperature fluctuations between night and day. Places of bountiful sustenance in one season, followed by up to three seasons of scarcity. Or places of bountiful sustenance with as much poison as nourishment, wearing the same subtle dressing, and requiring a still and attentive intimacy to know the difference.

Once, I slept on a mountain just east of Machu Picchu and dreamt I had the bald head of a vulture but huge rainbow wings that swept up suffering ancestors and sheltered them beneath long bright feathers.

▲▲▲▲

I wrote a poem about my paternal grandfather and father as maroons.

I wrote a poem about them fishing on the Santee Lake in South Carolina, their skin brown as the trees, their bones recognizing the swamp as safe refuge. One of the few places they could strip off their shirts and open their bare chests to the sun. Their feet in the cool water, dangling.

Were they free here? Like most poems, this story of my grandfather and father is make-believe but possibly true.

I have come to believe bones hold the earth element in our bodies. I have come to believe stones are ancestors. I have come to believe ancestors live in our bones, in the spongy nourishment of our marrow.

This is how I come to believe that this poem about my father and his grandfather is a real occurrence. I was there in the minds of the ancestors dreaming me forward into eventual being. I recognize the earth-memory in the marrow of my body.

It is possible that when I write poems like these, I am dreaming, and I have given my dreams a mountain to live on. To circumambulate in prayer.

▲▲▲▲

Maroon, which can have a more general sense of being abandoned without resources, entered English around the 1590s, from the French adjective marron, meaning feral or fugitive.

Fugitive: a person who is fleeing, as from prosecution, intolerable circumstances, etc.
Fugitive: fleeting; transitory; elusive.

Throughout the lands scarred by the Transatlantic Slave Trade, escaped enslaved people fled to the mountains to form maroon communities. One of the best-known quilombos (maroon settlements) in Brazil was Palmares (the Palm Nation), which was founded in the early seventeenth century throughout mountain ranges.

Maroon communities had to be inaccessible and were located in inhospitable environments to be sustainable.

At its height, Palmares had a population of over 30,000 free people, now called maroons, living towards a freedom that, by chain and whip, had been scarred into them as fantasy. But living it nonetheless.

▲▲▲▲

I can't say mountain without thinking fugitivity. Can't think fugitivity without thinking sanctuary. Can't think sanctuary without thinking home, rest, dream.

We are not always escaping. We are running towards as much as we are running away. We are believing, or daring to believe, or praying to believe in something we don't quite yet, in a future we want to be true.

What kind of humanity can hold such desperate faith?

It must be a special being who can reach so far into possibility. It must be a mind like silk thread, supple yet strong as steel, who can imagine towards the very edges of what is known without breaking. And then to step out with the body onto a road of pure conjecture...

What kind of humanity punishes such dreamers?

When maroons were recaptured by slave hunters (yes, that first iteration of police), the Achilles tendon would be cut, a leg amputated, a castration made public, a roasting made death.

When the Salvadoran "train" of asylum-seekers reaches the US border, the children are sifted from their parents to sleep wrapped in foil blankets, barbed wire, beneath gunpoint and uniformed cocks coming for them in the night.

That summer of 2018 in the Pisgahs, I learned there is an intersection of trails somewhere in the Great Smoky Mountains where a portion of the Underground Railroad overlaps with the Trail of Tears.

We dream routes to home. Sometimes the dreams are sorrow. The routes anguish, pushing up from our bodies, motoring one foot in front of the other on a dark road we don't know.

▲▲▲▲

When I drive now to Tamanowas Rock, older than the Cascades, it is another election year. The summer of 2020. On the short three mile drive I pass four Trump signs and three Blue Lives Matter flags. News has just surfaced that women in ICE custody have been given nonconsensual hysterectomies, forced sterilization, and yes, the children at the border are there, still.

My body lurches with such repetition. Is it possible that all time is a loop? How can four years have moved so much like rapid fire, yet so painstakingly slow? How can safety feel even farther away?

I go to Tamanowas Rock Sanctuary every week, my body tense on the drive and loosening once I pass the threshold to the trailhead.

I read of the mastodon hunters who perched its heights on lookout. I envision the dugout cedar canoes of the Coast Salish peoples tied with roots to Tamanowas during floods, waiting here safely until the waters receded.

I dream of ceremony and healing and prayer after prayer pattering this rock like rain, shaping it just as slowly.

This stone has stayed.

I wonder how many different kinds of humanity it has perceived in its lifetime. We come, we go, we collect and scatter like squirrels. Once, we pressed ourselves bare-skinned with barely any language against this rock, and now, we arrive in Gore-Tex with cell phones.

Leaning here, I try to get as quiet and still as forty-three million years.

I sit until I hear the far thunder heart and search in my own body for something that feels the same. Some rumbling lullaby in my most profound center that lets me think maybe I am also old. Maybe I am ancient. Maybe I too have something inside me so sturdy and robust that I can say, See? There is so much.

And open up my hands before me.

Acknowledgements

"Nine Winds (or, I am only ever writing about love)," *Green Mountains Review Vol. 32.1, April 2021.*

"A Discipline of Kindness," *The Willowherb Review, Issue 5, October 2022.*

"Sanctuary: Rock: Mountain: Home," *EcoTheo Collective Social Justice Folio, Autumn 2021.*

The formatting of "Shed" takes after "The Red Parakeet" by Lina María Ferreira Cabeza-Vanegas.

Many thanks to Sevé Torres and Muriel Leung for early, encouraging eyes on this little book. Gratitude to Bolo and to Wayne, the best road dogs a nomad-poet could ask for. And many thanks to Micheal Martone, for seeing what I hoped would be seen in this quirk of a memoir.

LISBETH WHITE lives on S'klallam and Chimacum land in the Pacific Northwest, where she writes towards eco-abolitionism and enchantivism. She is the author of the poetry collection, *American Sycamore* (Perugia Press, 2022), and co-editor of the anthology *Poetry as Spellcasting: Poems, Essays, and Prompts for Manifesting Liberation and Reclaiming Power* (North Atlantic Books, 2023). She has received support for her work from Artist Trust, VONA, Tin House, Roots. Wounds.Words., The Watering Hole, and Bread Loaf Environmental Writers Conference, as well as residencies with SeaSalted Honey, Blue Mountain Center and Bloedel Reserve.